Symbols, Landmarks, and Monuments

The
World Trade
Center

Tamara L. Britton
ABDO Publishing Company

visit us at
www.abdopub.com

Published by ABDO Publishing Company, 4940 Viking Drive, Edina, Minnesota 55435.
Copyright © 2003 by Abdo Consulting Group, Inc. International copyrights reserved in all countries. No part of this book may be reproduced in any form without written permission from the publisher.

Printed in the United States of America

Editors: Kate A. Conley, Kristy Langanki Cannon, Kristianne E. Vieregger
Photo Credits: AP/Wide World, Corbis, TimePix
Art Direction & Maps: Neil Klinepier

Library of Congress Cataloging-in-Publication Data

Britton, Tamara L., 1963-
    The World Trade Center / Tamara L. Britton.
        p. cm. -- (Symbols, landmarks and monuments)
    Includes index.
    Summary: Describes the history, design, construction, and original controversial nature of the World Trade Center, as well as the terrorist attack that destroyed it on September 11, 2001.
    ISBN 1-57765-850-7
    1. World Trade Center (New York, N.Y.)--Juvenile literature. 2. Skyscrapers--New York (State)--New York--Juvenile literature. 3. New York (N.Y.)--Buildings, structures, etc.--Juvenile literature. [1. World Trade Center (New York, N.Y.) 2. Skyscrapers.] I. Title.

NA6233.N5 B73 2002
720'.483'097471--dc21
                                                                    2002025357

Contents

The World Trade Center 4

Fun Facts 6

Timeline 7

The Beginnings 8

Preparing the Site 12

Building the World Trade Center 16

A Symbol of Pride 26

September 11, 2001 30

The Future of the World Trade Center 34

Glossary 38

Web Sites 39

Index 40

The World Trade Center

For 30 years, the World Trade Center stood as a symbol of U.S. **capitalism** and **democracy**. At first, many people disliked the World Trade Center buildings. But over time, the towers grew to define New York and the Manhattan skyline.

Then, on September 11, 2001, the World Trade Center was destroyed in an act of **terrorism**. Thousands of people from all over the world were killed. And one of America's greatest **landmarks** was lost.

The twin towers of the World Trade Center defined the Manhattan skyline.

The World Trade Center's **lease** owner has vowed to rebuild it. The new World Trade Center will rise from the site where two of the world's most famous buildings once stood. The story of their construction shows persistence, political disagreements, and cutting-edge engineering.

Aerial view of Manhattan

Fun Facts

√ The World Trade Center cost $575 million to build.

√ Eight thousand people worked on its construction.

√ Many historical items were excavated from the building site. They included seventeenth-century ship anchors, cannonballs, glass vessels, and coins.

√ During construction, a massive steel panel was accidentally dropped from a helicopter into the Kill Van Kull Channel, where it remains today.

√ The towers contained 200,000 tons (181,000 t) of steel; 6 million feet (1,830,000 m) of walls; 5 million square feet (465,000 sq. m) of painted surfaces; 1,520 miles (2,446 km) of wire; and 7 million square feet (650,000 sq. m) of tile.

√ The towers had 43,600 windows; 254 elevators; and 200,000 light fixtures.

√ The air conditioning system in the towers was powerful enough to cool 15,000 homes.

√ About 50,000 of the 3 million people who commute into Manhattan on weekdays worked at the World Trade Center.

√ Engineers determined that people inside could comfortably tolerate the towers slowly swaying a distance of 11 inches (28 cm).

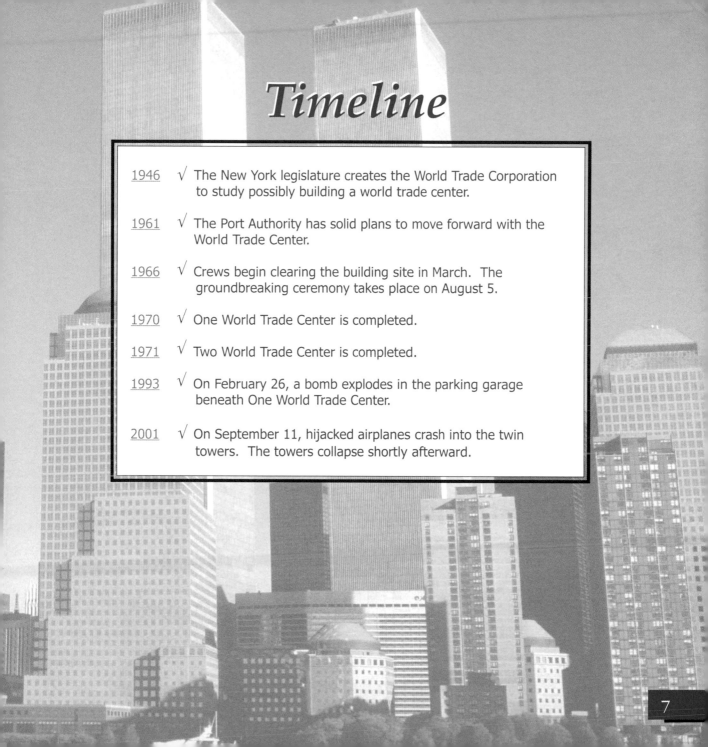

Timeline

<u>1946</u> √	The New York legislature creates the World Trade Corporation to study possibly building a world trade center.
<u>1961</u> √	The Port Authority has solid plans to move forward with the World Trade Center.
<u>1966</u> √	Crews begin clearing the building site in March. The groundbreaking ceremony takes place on August 5.
<u>1970</u> √	One World Trade Center is completed.
<u>1971</u> √	Two World Trade Center is completed.
<u>1993</u> √	On February 26, a bomb explodes in the parking garage beneath One World Trade Center.
<u>2001</u> √	On September 11, hijacked airplanes crash into the twin towers. The towers collapse shortly afterward.

The Beginnings

World War II destroyed many of the world's major cities. But no battles occurred in the United States, so its cities were not destroyed. For this reason, many foreign businesses moved to the United States after the war.

During this time, businesses in the United States produced half of the world's goods. Many of these businesses worked together and wanted to be located near each other. So in 1946, the New York **legislature** created the World Trade Corporation. This organization studied the possibility of building a world trade center.

The project turned out to be too big to undertake. But many people still liked the idea of a world trade center. In 1959, businessman David Rockefeller decided he wanted to improve lower Manhattan. So he built the 60-story Chase Manhattan Bank Building.

David Rockefeller

This model shows plans for a lower Manhattan building project in 1955. The white structure is the proposed Chase Manhattan Bank Building.

9

The bank, though, did not generate enough business to revive the area. So Rockefeller formed a new business organization. He called it the Downtown-Lower Manhattan Association (DLMA). The DLMA came up with a plan to improve lower Manhattan. The plan included building a world trade center.

Rockefeller knew it would take a powerful group to undertake such a large project. So he gave the plan to the **Port Authority** of New York and New Jersey to study.

In 1961, the Port Authority outlined a solid plan for the World Trade Center. Austin Tobin, the director of the Port Authority, created the World Trade Office in 1962. It would plan, develop, construct, and operate the World Trade Center.

Erecting two of the world's tallest buildings proved to be a difficult task.

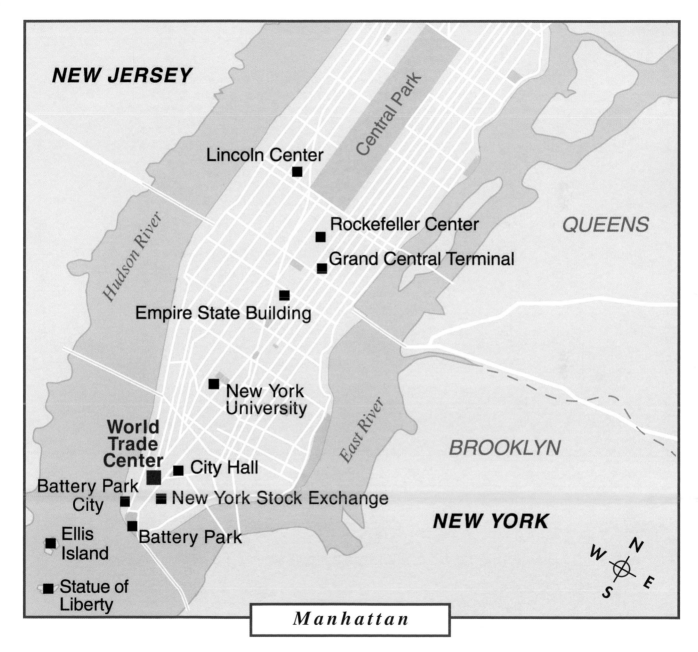

NEW JERSEY

Central Park

QUEENS

Hudson River

Lincoln Center

Rockefeller Center

Grand Central Terminal

Empire State Building

New York University

East River

BROOKLYN

World Trade Center

City Hall

Battery Park City

New York Stock Exchange

NEW YORK

Ellis Island

Battery Park

Statue of Liberty

N
W   E
S

Manhattan

Preparing the Site

The **Port Authority** chose **architect** Minoru Yamasaki to design the World Trade Center. Port Authority officials wanted a place where people could work, as well as enjoy themselves. Yamasaki's design included two tall towers and five shorter buildings surrounding a **plaza**.

The Port Authority chose the land in lower Manhattan on which to build the World Trade Center. More than a thousand businesses, offices, and residences occupied the land. The people who worked and lived there did not want to move. They thought the Port Authority was not paying them enough for their losses.

A group of business owners **sued** the Port Authority to stop the project. But in 1963, the U.S. Supreme Court ruled against them. This meant the existing buildings could be torn down.

Minoru Yamasaki with his World Trade Center model

The **Port Authority** presented plans to the public in 1964. Two 110-story towers would boast 10 million square feet (930,000 sq. m) of office space. The project was estimated to cost $350 million.

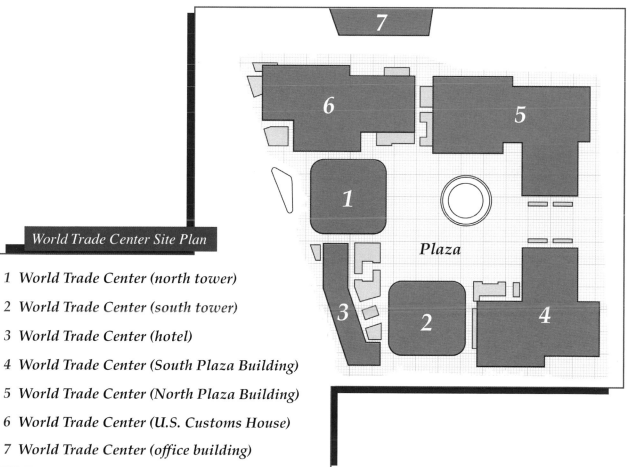

Plaza

World Trade Center Site Plan

1 *World Trade Center (north tower)*

2 *World Trade Center (south tower)*

3 *World Trade Center (hotel)*

4 *World Trade Center (South Plaza Building)*

5 *World Trade Center (North Plaza Building)*

6 *World Trade Center (U.S. Customs House)*

7 *World Trade Center (office building)*

Many people opposed the plan. Some thought it was too expensive. Others thought the towers would disrupt TV and radio reception. Still others feared that the twin towers would collapse, crushing everything around them. Business leaders thought the huge amount of office space in the towers would lower rental values in Manhattan.

The **Port Authority** had another obstacle to overcome. The project was located in the Port Authority's **jurisdiction**. So New York City would not be able to collect taxes on the rental space. This upset the city's mayor.

The mayor demanded that the Port Authority agree to make yearly payments to the city. The payments would make up for the lost tax money. Until then, the mayor refused to close the streets running through the 16-acre (6-ha) construction site.

So the **Port Authority** agreed to pay taxes to New York City on the space rented to private tenants. It also agreed to use the earth removed from the construction site to create new land. About 100 acres (40 ha) of new land would be built along the edge of Manhattan in the Hudson River. This new land would generate much tax money for New York City.

With these issues finally settled, construction began. The groundbreaking ceremony took place on August 5, 1966. Construction crews quickly went to work.

The towers were especially breathtaking when lit up at night.

Building the World Trade Center

The World Trade Center had an unusual design. The outside walls, rather than interior columns, carried the building's weight. The only interior columns were the elevator shafts. Yamasaki managed this by spacing the **vertical** steel columns of the outside walls close together.

Yamasaki's design created wide, open office spaces. They did not have floor-to-ceiling support columns. The design also allowed the building to withstand winds of 150 miles per hour (241 km/h)!

Another of Yamasaki's design features was the elevator system. A regular elevator system would take up too much space inside the building. So Yamasaki used the Sky Lobby system.

In the system, he divided the building into three parts, called zones. Each zone had a lobby. Lobbies were located on the first, forty-first, and seventy-second floors. Passengers exited an elevator at the lobby. Then they crossed the lobby, got on another elevator, and rode it up to the next zone. This system allowed for the most possible usable space in the building.

In March 1966, crews began clearing the 16-acre (6-ha) site. After the site was cleared, underground **utility lines** were rerouted. Then 1.2 million cubic yards (917,000 cu. m) of earth had to be moved in order to lay the **foundation**.

The World Trade Center Elevator System

■ *Express Elevators*

□ *Local Elevators*

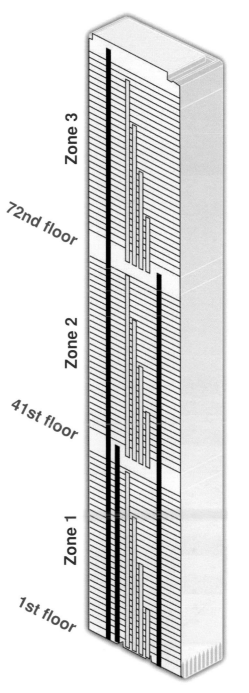

Zone 3

72nd floor

Zone 2

41st floor

Zone 1

1st floor

The earth removed from the site was dumped into a box in the Hudson River. This new land became Battery Park City and the World Financial Center.

After completing the **foundations**, construction crews began building the twin towers. First, they constructed the elevator shafts. Then, they built the outside walls, including the strong outer columns. Next, they built the floors. Finally, workers sprayed the building with **flame-retardant** material and covered it with steel panels.

The construction site was quite small. So building materials were stored in New Jersey. Workers brought the materials to Manhattan as they were needed. The construction work had to be well organized. If the next required building material was not there when needed, construction was delayed.

Construction on the towers is finally underway.

Some of the steel columns used in the building weighed more than 50 tons (45 t). Boats, helicopters, and trucks brought them across the river from New Jersey. Construction workers used huge cranes to lift the steel sections up as the building rose.

Workers completed One World Trade Center, the north tower, in 1970. It had 110 stories and was 1,368 feet (417 m) tall. Workers completed Two World Trade Center, the south tower, in 1971. It had 110 stories and was 1,362 feet (415 m) tall.

The official **dedication** of the World Trade Center took place on April 4, 1973. At that time, the twin towers were the world's tallest buildings.

Construction continued on the rest of the World Trade Center buildings. Six World Trade Center opened in 1973. It housed the U.S. Customs Service. Three World Trade Center, a 23-story hotel, opened in 1981. Seven World Trade Center was built in 1987.

21

The World Trade Center held more than just offices. A shopping mall was located beneath the towers. There was also a police station, a Federal Aviation Administration (FAA) communication center, a telephone station, and a parking garage.

The tops of the towers also had much to offer. The top of

Two World Trade Center had an **observation deck**. The top of One World Trade Center had the world-class Windows on the World restaurant.

After decades of work and planning, the world finally had a place to **consolidate** its **economic** business in the United States.

The Windows on the World restaurant offered diners spectacular views of the city.

A Symbol of Pride

At first, many people disliked the World Trade Center. The towers were not designed in a familiar style. And people thought the twin towers were too big.

Slowly, though, people began to accept the towers. They enjoyed the view from the **observation deck**. They liked the fine dining and beautiful sunsets at Windows on the World.

Soon, the towers became a symbol of New York City and lower Manhattan. The World Trade Center had become a center of the world **economy** and American **capitalism**. Americans and New Yorkers were proud of the World Trade Center and what it represented.

The World Trade Center lobbies were wide-open spaces. Each day, thousands of people who visited or worked in the towers passed through these lobbies.

Some people, however, didn't like what the World Trade Center represented. A few of them believed **terrorism** was the best way to express how they felt. On February 26, 1993, at 12:18 P.M., an explosion rocked One World Trade Center. It killed six people and injured more than a thousand others. The explosion was the worst act of terrorism ever in the United States at the time.

Investigators quickly determined that a bomb had been hidden in a van. The van was parked next to a support column in the tower's underground parking lot. Whoever had planted the bomb had been trying to topple the tower.

Soon, investigators found a piece of the van. It had an identification number on it. This number led to Mohammad Salameh. A search of Salameh's apartment led investigators to a storage facility.

The storage facility contained explosives and bomb-making materials. Those items matched evidence taken from the World Trade Center. Police officers arrested Salameh and three other individuals. The terrorists were tried, convicted, and sent to prison.

Firefighters and rescue workers respond to the site of the 1993 bombing.

September 11, 2001

After the 1993 bombing, workers repaired the World Trade Center. Engineers worked long days for many weeks. It cost more than $500 million to repair the damage. The underground parking garage remained closed. But most of the World Trade Center's tenants resumed business as usual.

Construction workers repair the damage after the 1993 bombing.

The twin towers remained a target for those who opposed American **capitalism** and **democracy**. On Tuesday, September 11, 2001, airplanes crashed into the World Trade Center's twin towers. At 8:45 A.M., American Airlines Flight 11 hit One World Trade Center. At 9:03 A.M., United Airlines Flight 175 hit Two World Trade Center.

Both of the planes had taken off from Boston, Massachusetts, and were headed for

Among the wreckage is an outdoor memorial dedicated to the victims of the 1993 bombing.

Workers quickly begin clearing the debris after the terrorist attack.

Los Angeles, California. They each contained about 20,000 gallons (76,000 liters) of fuel. Inside the towers, heat from the burning jet fuel reached 2,000 degrees Fahrenheit (1,093° C).

The fire's intense heat melted the outer steel columns that supported the weight of the buildings. Without the outer columns, the towers collapsed.

Two World Trade Center collapsed at 9:59 A.M. At 10:28 A.M., One World Trade Center fell. Debris from the towers fell onto the other World Trade Center buildings, causing severe damage. Many other buildings near the World Trade Center were also destroyed.

It had taken more than two decades to plan and build the World Trade Center. In less than two hours, it was gone. In its place stood a nine-story pile of debris, and 10,000 tons (9,000 t) of ash and soot. The world struggled to understand what had caused this tragedy.

A Chain Reaction

①

The massive impact of the airplane crashing through several floors weakened the tower. Thousands of gallons of fuel from the airplane caught on fire. The fire melted the tower's steel support columns.

②

One of the tower's concrete floors may have pulled away from the steel support columns when they melted during the fire.

③

The force of concrete floors smashing into one another set off a "pancake" effect. This made the tower collapse rather than topple to the side.

The Future of the World Trade Center

On September 11, 2001, President George W. Bush announced that the United States had been the target of a **terrorist** attack. Nineteen men had **hijacked** four planes. They used the planes to strike American **landmarks** and monuments.

In addition to the tragedy at the World Trade Center, another plane struck the Pentagon near Washington, D.C. Yet another plane crashed in a Pennsylvania field. Its passengers had attacked the hijackers so they would not crash the plane into another building.

The 19 hijackers were believed to be part of al-Qaeda. It is a terrorist group run by Osama bin Laden. Bin Laden and his followers were upset that the United States

Osama bin Laden

Without the World Trade Center,
Manhattan's skyline appears empty.

had soldiers stationed in Saudi Arabia. They also did not like U.S. support of Israel.

Al-Qaeda **terrorists** try to gain support for their causes by scaring citizens. The terrorists hope that frightened citizens will beg their governments to give in to terrorist demands in order to stop the violence.

But their plan on September 11 did not work. The world stood by the United States as President Bush declared war on terrorism. A group of countries worked together to bring to justice the terrorists who destroyed the World Trade Center.

Meanwhile, people continued to mourn for those who had died. Exactly six months after the attack, a **memorial** called Tribute in Light was lit near the World Trade Center site. It was made up of two beams of light. They represented the fallen towers. The lights shone at night for 32 days.

Many people also focused on plans to rebuild the World Trade Center. The **Port Authority** of New York and New Jersey owned the World Trade Center. In July 2001, the Port Authority granted Larry Silverstein a 99-year **lease** on the property.

After the attack, Silverstein vowed to rebuild the World Trade Center. The new World Trade Center will have a **memorial** for the thousands who lost their lives in the tragic destruction of one of America's most famous **landmarks**.

Tribute in Light was lit on March 11, 2002.

Glossary

architect - a person who plans and designs buildings.

capitalism - an economic system where businesses compete to sell their products and services.

consolidate - to combine together into one unit.

dedication - a ceremony that officially sets aside a building for a specific use.

democracy - a governmental system in which the people vote on how to run the country.

economy - the way a nation uses its money, goods, and natural resources.

flame-retardant - resists burning or starting on fire.

foundation - an underlying support structure or base in a building.

hijack - to overtake a vehicle, such as an airplane, by threatening the pilot with violence.

jurisdiction - an area where a particular group has the power to govern or enforce laws.

landmark - an important structure of historical or physical interest.

lease - a rental contract.

legislature - a group of people given the power to make laws.

memorial - something that stands as a reminder of a person or event.

observation deck - an area near the top of a building where people can go to see a view of the city.

plaza - a public square or open area, often with trees and shrubs and places to sit.

Port Authority - a public organization that controls and manages transportation facilities such as bridges, tunnels, and airports, as well as other structures.

sue - to bring a person or organization to court.

terrorist - a person who uses violence to threaten people or governments. This kind of violence is called terrorism.

utility lines - lines for services such as electricity or water.

vertical - in the up-and-down position.

World War II - 1939 to 1945, fought in Europe, Asia, and Africa. The United States, France, Great Britain, the Soviet Union, and their allies were on one side. Germany, Italy, Japan, and their allies were on the other side. The war began when Germany invaded Poland. The United States entered the war in 1941 after Japan bombed Pearl Harbor, Hawaii.

Web Sites

Would you like to learn more about the World Trade Center? Please visit **www.abdopub.com** to find up-to-date Web site links with models, drawings, and photographs of the World Trade Center. These links are routinely monitored and updated to provide the most current information available.

Index

A

al-Qaeda 34, 36

B

Battery Park City 18
bin Laden, Osama 34
Boston, Massachusetts 30
Bush, George W. 34, 36

C

Chase Manhattan Bank
    Building 8
construction 5, 10, 15, 17,
    18, 20
Customs Service, U.S. 20

D

Downtown-Lower
    Manhattan Association
    10

F

Federal Aviation
    Administration 22

H

Hudson River 15, 18

I

Israel 36

L

Los Angeles, California 32

M

Manhattan, New York City
    4, 8, 10, 12, 14, 15, 18,
    26
memorials 36, 37

N

New Jersey 18, 20
New York 4, 8, 26
New York City, New York
    14, 15, 26

O

observation deck 22, 26
One World Trade Center
    20, 22, 28, 30, 32

P

Pennsylvania 34
Pentagon 34
Port Authority of New York
    and New Jersey 10,
    12, 13, 14, 15, 36

R

Rockefeller, David 8, 10

S

Salameh, Mohammad 28
Saudi Arabia 36
Seven World Trade Center
    20
Silverstein, Larry 36, 37
Six World Trade Center 20
Sky Lobby system 16, 17
Supreme Court, U.S. 12

T

terrorist attacks 4, 28, 30,
    32, 34, 36
Three World Trade Center
    20
Tobin, Austin 10
Tribute in Light 36
Two World Trade Center
    20, 22, 30, 32

W

Washington, D.C. 34
Windows on the World 22,
    26
World Financial Center 18
World Trade Corporation 8
World Trade Office 10
World War II 8

Y

Yamasaki, Minoru 12, 16